Photograph: Thee Walker

Ian McBryde was born in Toronto, Canada, in 1953, and has lived in Australia since coming for a year's holiday in 1972. During that time, he has been engaged in a diversity of occupations — including truck driver, illustrator, computer data supervisor, and drummer for various Melbourne bands.

His poetry has been published in Australia and overseas. *The Familiar* is his first collection.

■ CONTEMPORARY AUSTRALIAN POETS

The Familiar

Ian McBryde

Hale & Iremonger

For Jordie Patricia Albiston

Acknowledgements

Blue Jacket (Japan), *Bogg* (USA), *Bystander*, *Chelsea Hotel* (Germany), *Labyrinth* (Canada), *Next Exit* (Canada), *Nocturnal Submissions*, *The Perseverance Anthology*, *Roads* (UK), *The Small Times*, *Tempus Fugit* (Belgium), *Vehicle*, 3RRR (Melbourne), 3CCC (Central Victoria), Channel 31, SKA Television (Melbourne), and Channel 19, Cambridge Cable TV (Boston).

Typeset, printed & bound by
Southwood Press Pty Limited
80–92 Chapel Street, Marrickville, NSW

For the publisher
Hale & Iremonger Pty Limited
GPO Box 2552, Sydney, NSW

National Library of Australia Cataloguing-in-Publication entry

McBryde, Ian, 1953-
  The Familiar.

  ISBN 0 86806 519 6.

  I. Title. (Series: Contemporary Australian poets).

A821.3

Publication of this title was assisted by the Australia Council, the Federal Government's arts funding and advisory body

Front Cover: Photograph by the author

Contents

ARRIVE

with your black columns
your shadow bell
your squeaky legions.

Trail your thick cape
over my sleepless face,
let its soft grey hem
slip across my lips.

Pull the moon down
into this damp jungle.
Present me with that
which leopards smell:

the coming of hunters
the message of weather
the scent of gazelles.

SATELLITE

There will never be an end
to this vast circle
that I make around you.

Past mathematics
my rapid transit
across your quiet sky
is certain as night.

Held like tides
I lean into this ageless curve
a rocketing, burning magnet
angling through the blackness.

Below, on your surface
nothing alters
but with each pass

you stir in your core
aware of me out there
orbiting, orbiting.

MOON

Predatory, acne-wracked
white criminal

blind eye
widening into the night
a venomous

shrunken nun
spilling thin, shrill light.

Her dead stare carries
no vestige of salvation
as she rides

the rain's tail
the nameless waves
the black back of magic.

OUTPATIENT

His is a portable bedlam
with the shrieks hidden
inside, where everything fits.

Under his skin are fingers
scrabbling at walls
plucking at rubber.

Past his bland smile
are manacles and hoses
and the stench of disinfectant.

Behind those eyes is a door
with a reinforced window
he can rush tightfisted at.

There is no handle on his side.
This seems to amuse him.
In his thin laughter

you can hear sirens rising
shrill and insistent
to a terrible pitch.

BLACKHOUSE

A reek of dust.
Elevators
that never descend.
Back stairs

broken banisters
landings in shadow.
Doors partially ajar
off featureless halls.

This is where
the helpless register,
where the muted
come to stay. They

will appreciate
the fine warning
the marks on the wall
and the barricade

to the top floor:
the inexplicable sounds
and the nightly
mad flap of pigeons

rising in filthy clouds
from the roof.
The muted too
will understand

that at last they are
back, they are
home. Home
to the vacancy

to the unchanged place.
Home to the shredded
hopes. The cold room.
The red zone.

LIONESS

In distant
empty mansions
you pad soundlessly
down halls of moss

lean head swivelling
a hunting moan
low in your throat.

Pulse. Scent.
No warning.
Stillness, then

the flicker.
The ripple of shoulders.
The shivering, golden moment.

[12]

THE FIFTH SEASON

Through a gap
at the back of winter
is the fifth season.
From its bleak hills

the flocks rise
in a glittery
screeching wheel.
Aloft, their cries die away.
Everywhere is south
nowhere is south: their
frantic shadows blacken
the valley floor. We take

our places on the terrace,
I near the windows
you there at the balcony.

A final frost crosses
our marble faces,
your alabaster hand
rests on the railing.
Already we are
beyond weather.
Everything
has been said.

Our stone throats close
over a tragic alphabet:
ice and lies and silence
the anguished, last language
of statues.

WRONG NUMBER

Hello
who is it hello.

An echo
an antarctica shifting
ground down
a continent edging away.

Muttering.
The words fused, snatches.
Around three.
She'll be asleep.
Can't see without her glasses.

Who is it hello.
A frozen humming
through the wires
another voice
I'm ready.
Meet you outside.
Let's get it over with.

Who's that hello hello.
Is there someone there.
A clicking
a distant hiss

as the glacier wakes.
Is there anyone there
hello who is it
hello hello hello

REVENGE

Diners are swallowing their last mouthfuls
as he enters the crowded cafe
his brain a bright desert his heart
a scarred, night tundra.

Sweat inches down his ribs
as he clicks off the safety.
Now his thoughts shimmer like mirages
as the weapon appears from beneath his coat.

Back home he has left all the lights on
and the two dogs he will never see again
shiver together in the tiny kitchen
bruised and hungry, awaiting his return.

CAT TO ANTELOPE

That's it. Graze away
unwary, just far enough
apart from the herd.

Flick your ears.
Watch the trees.

I'm silent and still
and more patient than you.
It's nearly night.

There's no wind.
I can stay for hours like this.

THERE ARE OTHERS

'They will just replace me. There are others.'
— David Berkowitz, alleged 'Son of Sam' killer, New York, 1977

Cowled, they gather
in clearings
at the back of caves
in the black
and abandoned places.

The date will matter,
has been planned in advance.
A forest of torches
singes the winter air:

in Brooklyn
someone has two hours to live.
Echoes of the final chant
roll into a still night.

At last. Now down
to the forbidden.
Invocation. Red sex.

Ritual.
Maybe later
a snuff film.

21ST CENTURY ZODIAC

The sign of the ad break.
The sign of death on camera.
The sign of the hollow weekend.
The sign of shattered families.
The sign of the laser.
The sign of corroded honour.
The sign of the cybernaut.
The sign of the empty house.
The sign of body armour.
The sign of the transferred call.
The sign of movement in shadow.
The sign of the crouching sniper.

AMERICAN PSYCHE

News at seven news at eleven.
We'll term it murder rule it
suicide let television judge
with its grim syntax
its gunshot punctuation.

Newsprint twists
down back alleys
headlines illegible.

We will never know.
We will never have
enough of substance

to fill up this Memphis
this Los Angeles
this Dealey Plaza of the soul.

DALLAS '63

(Under sleeping seas
the net spreads taut
and ready for its grim haul
there is barely a ripple.)

1. *Zapruder Footage*

Pink mist.
In endless replays
his head
snaps backwards
over and over she
scrambles onto the trunk
for his scalp.
Sirens wind up
as the limo accelerates.

2. *Camera 7, NBC*

Lenses held
on the hospital doors.
Confusion orderlies police
close-ups of people weeping.

3. *KRLD-TV Interview*

Q: Did you shoot the president.
A: I didn't shoot anybody sir.
  I haven't been told
  what I'm here for.
Q: Do you have a lawyer.
A: No sir I don't.

4. *Camera 3, CBS*

Oswald, held at the elbows
snarling the truth back
over his shoulder, 'A patsy
I'm just a patsy'.

5. *Camera 8, ABC*

Oswald
battered and sullen
led down corridors
by grim-faced agents:
Ruby pushes
through the hall of cops
fires his smuggled-in gun.
The dying grimace
wins every slot
on prime time.

6. *Off-camera*

Virginia;
men in suits nod to each other.

Havana;
glasses are raised in a toast.

Chicago;
chairs pushed back from the table.

Marseilles;
radios retuned to music.

New Orleans they sigh with relief
turn off the t.v. leave
separately not speaking (under
sleeping seas the net

[21]

tightens closes.
There is barely a sliver
of moon to illuminate
the mute, minute
diminishing

ripples).

ELEMENTAL

Back to water.
Like those drowned
our mouths
sound out the shoal
our sightless eyes
plumb its cold slopes.
We sink slowly, gently
turning in the current.

Back to fire.
Silent and patient, we wait
in the appointed place.
Our shadows waver
harden. Some of us
have come great distances,
none of us can return.
So we stay awake.
Guard our wood.
Pray for rain.

Back to earth.
A surfacing through stone,
the first breath pebbles.
Dust on us
our limbs thinned
with lack of use
caked in hibernation.

Back to air.
Wings gone when we wake;
the nest a memory
the brilliant peaks
almost forgotten.
Claw marks.
A muskiness.
Feathers in the bed.

[23]

ONTARIO CALLING

Above the treeline
a wolf pack circles
alert, slit-eyed
snouts lifted
into the evening breeze.

New moon. The loons
triple their lost cries
across the water.

Autumn stalks the shore
long before dawn
under a wide sky gone
unimaginably black.

The island is quiet.
The lake is waiting.
Beneath its surface
the patient weeds
reach up for me.

THE SILK ONE

Under your sleeping face
beneath the softness
and the low breath
and the closed red lips

I sometimes sense
that ancestry of bandits
through which you hasten,
stepping over the sentry's blood

and scaling
the naked wall, blade
between your teeth
a fierce grin

keeping those red lips back
from its pitted
brilliant
edge.

THE FAMILIAR

No crow no black cat
just you

waiting in every room
of the last house I'll visit.

One thread drawing me in
one hidden exit

between worlds.
I am nearing the corner.

The street greets me
like a fond, lost son.

The house porches out
to receive me

its mirrors
ready their secrets.

My key in the door.
My feet on the stairs.

My reflection in glass
for the last time.

THE BLOOD JET

Disguised I
trace contour maps
and vapour trails.
Where will it descend,
in what black city?

I know when I'm close.
I have a nose for cordite.
Dressed as a mechanic
I shall sidle through
as the hangar opens.

No-one will notice
when I climb the ladder
and strap myself in.

I could sleep alright
after that flight.

I could outrun night itself
with my hands on those controls.

KAMIKAZE

Below us
just under the summer clouds
the great ships wait
plump and unsuspecting.

Soon we shall fall
from the morning sky.

We take the ancient lie
translate it into flame
and stealth and fuselage;
the targets expanding
frantic, as we drop.

There is just enough fuel
to get here and circle briefly.
They have not taught us
how to land.

Death chants fill our cabin.
Blood streams from our ears.

Divine winds guide us down
spiralling, triumphant
into the guns' bright muzzles.

AVIARY

for Alex Skovron

The sound of wings
fills my small room,
a fluttering
frantic elegance
a concert of feathers and air.

We beat against the same glass
yearning for immediacy
for a flight replete with healing.

Outside the sky
has already escaped.
Still within, thirsty
undeterred, we all beat
against the same glass.

CHET BAKER'S FACE

Gaunt as autumn
beautifully cruel
each wrinkle a lonely road
there was no reversing down.

Even in youth
sneering into the microphone
the same doom rippled
grim and sinuous
across his features.

Perhaps he felt
his crawl through hell
well worth it:
each time he was revived
nursed frantically back
from smack heaven
came his laconic comment
chill-dried *Hey man*
you wrecked my high.

FEVER IN DEVON

Unimaginable, the blackness
slapping at the heels
of your unique delirium:
the sweat-drenched nights
rolled back, packed
into your tightening heart
all pump and shudder
unlikely as dynamite.

Outside the cottage
death set in
like inevitable weather,
uncoiled his fuses
threaded them around
your avenues of escape.

All he had to do then
was sit back and await
the woman who got
too close, in whose hand

was the stolen key
over whose radiant
face was draped
the veil of flames.

REPORTS FROM THE PALACE

For days the soldiers
have been dragging the moat.
Our questions are met
with sullen stares.

*

The bridge is up
the hunt is cancelled.
No-one is allowed out.

*

Closed windows
behind an empty throne.
Masks on the wall.
The hush of tapestries.
Anything could happen now.

*

Friday
we see lights
in the south tower.

*

From upstairs we can watch
the untended maze
growing slowly inward
closing itself off.

*

Grass is growing
where the children ran.

*

After the banquet
when we are excused
certain ones stay back.

*

Mud
in the front hall.
Someone has been outside.

*

[32]

Late and very faintly
we hear music
from the south tower.

*

They are keeping us longer
at assembly.
We must be careful.

*

Sunday night
your message got through.
No one noticed.

*

It is arranged.
Just meet me
where we agreed.

*

The guard is doubled;
they are whispering
on the ground floor.

*

Not allowed downstairs.
Locked in after dark.

*

Our quarters are searched
nothing is found.

*

I have been practising.
I will not be missed
before morning.

*

Masks.
Tapestries.
The south tower.

*

Anything could happen now.

[33]

TREASURE HUNT

Impact. Bejewelled with glass
her slim hands
reach over the twisting wheel.

Luminescent, serene
her features flower
through carats of windshield:

eyes a mine of rich silver
hair a riot of diamonds
throat a blossoming necklace

of rubies. She is almost smiling.
Strong, bright orchestras
herald her flight through the last

few priceless feet of air.

FIRST WATCH

I celebrate
that perfect face
raised to the light
that last glance
as you vanish.

I patrol the door you close.
There is no key
but I have the password. It is
WAIT FOR ME.

I nearly believe you.
I reel, delirious
at the thought of your return.

Even now I almost
want your voice to surface

still almost wish your kisses
could reach down this far.

[35]

BRETT WHITELEY DEAD

He slips his leash
one cold June Tuesday
and his friends
reminisce on television.
Heads shaken
heroin mentioned
and the camera pans in
on those familiar images:

the pallid hand
the dripping syringe
the wolf-monkey
slavering with impatience.

They speak of your habit
but not your hunger
and never of the presence
of the pale one
who walked alongside
with his sly white gift;
the guide who led you
to the powder world

took you
too far in this time
and lost you
let you go to sleep
and keep on going.

VISCERAL

Everything is true down here.
I built this pit to last
each stake placed lovingly

just so, points facing up.
I don't even need camouflage.
You'll come, clean and eager

to my edge and leap
dying each time on my spikes
but with no pain, beautifully.

JACK CITY

Give us
your huddled masses
your teeming millions

yearning to be free;
we'll issue them
with the dead hope

of television
with semi-automatics
and crack and by god

and all that's white
we'll see to it
that they fade away

in undefended lobbies
in broken doorways
that they perish

in tenements
and subways
and filthy streets we'll

attend to details
keep the books
look out for them

they'll be included
we'll tell both sides
we know what's

right just
trust us we'll
see to it.

[38]

HIGH UP IN CRIMSON

'No sense makes sense.'
— Charles Manson, Los Angeles, 1969

1. Spahn Ranch, August 8, 1969, 11:30 P.M.

Charlie alone
waits on the boardwalk
knee-deep
in his surf of fear
watching the receding tail-lights
of Johnny Swartz's Ford.

The trusted ones leaving
cleave into a quiet night
not actually laughing
but excited, fired up
whispering.

Legend has it
the last thing Charlie says
is to leave something witchy.

2. Benedict Canyon, August 9, 12:15 A.M.

They scale the gate, palms sweaty
ready for what's next.
From first shot to last stab
the whole thing
takes less than twenty minutes.

Spattered, they clamber back into the car
unified, entire.
Their bloody clothing's bundled up
thrown down a hillside.

They are singing.
Back at the ranch
Sadie scrubs smudges off the Ford.

3. Benedict Canyon, August 9, 4:50 A.M.

Charlie and one of the others
creep into Cielo Drive.
They wipe the place of prints
arrange the dead
in an unsuccessful tableau
and then replace them.

As they leave the still house
Charlie deliberately drops
a pawnshop pair of glasses
the cops will spend
fruitless months investigating.

4. Benedict Canyon, August 9, 8:30 A.M

The maid comes in the service entrance
finds the bodies
runs down the hill screaming.

Within minutes the house
is bursting with police
some of whom leave
fresh red heelmarks on the porch.

5. Spahn Ranch, August 9, 6:00 P.M.

A few of them
are watching t.v. in the trailer.
Sadie and Katie giggle
when the murders are mentioned.

[40]

6. Los Feliz, August 9, 11:45 P.M.

Six of them depart in the Ford
take to the freeways
end up in the valley.

Charlie picks a house, goes in
ties the people up and reassures them
then returns to the car.

The six split up: some drive off
and the others go inside.
It lasts five or six minutes.
High up in crimson
on the living room wall
they write RISE.

Afterwards they grab
some chocolate milk from the fridge
and hitch back to the ranch.

7. Spahn Ranch, August 10, 3:15 A.M.

The family sleeps.
Charlie paces the boardwalk alone
knowing he's falling.

It's all come true.
It's all expanded
past that which was intended.

The desert
stretches out in his head:
endless, beckoning
an edgeless refuge.

8. San Quentin

Charlie remains in solitary.
He has to: they keep
trying him out.

One inmate doused him
with paint thinner
lit him up. Everyone watched
not moving, while Charlie
writhed on the workshop floor
smothering the flames himself.

Charlie still gets
hundreds of letters a week
that he no longer needs to read.

While the others sleep
Charlie waits and listens,
ear to the night
coming to Now.
Silently, coyotes
rush down a gulch inside him.
Apparently Charlie
never made a sound
when he moved.

He likes that we remember this.

On visiting days the guards
escort the well-connected
slowly past his cell.

I WANT YOU ELECTRIC

I demand the snapped current
the shattered transformer
the broken pole

I need falling neon
split trees on innocent streets
the fine ash of power stations

I embrace the late ambulance
the blacked out panic
the frantic call

I want your lightning
up my spine I want
you shaking with fever

alive with shock god
how I want you
electric.

24 HOURS

We are drenched, shipwrecked
out of a sea of sheets
beached on each other.

Your room is a welcome dune
silent and still.
Moonlight dusts us
with her lingering passage.

Asleep your lips form
the clues of a new language
a dream dialect.

The cat's ears prick up.
We lie in the dark, listening.

Much later he wakes me
purring, as he licks you
off my fingers.

INSIDE

her I'm one
with the velvet

the wet the soft fog

the call we all
flock to the call

beyond speech the deep

hum the rumble
the ultimate

shudder.

[45]

PANTHERS

Encaged, we pace
our trampled circuit
ears flattened
flanks shaking with rage
whiskers brushing the bars.

We are never far
from the kingdom of screams.

Do you think us gentle
almost docile
as we doze in the quiet heat?

Asleep, all we dream of
is prey in the forests
with our quarry's blood
punching out narcotic rhythms
of fear, and mindless flight.

The ecstasy of such hunting
blunts all but our wicked claws
our victim's rictus
our red snarl of victory.

IN COUNTRY

Still jungle.
Back in The World
twenty-two years
still jungle every night.

Five a.m.
The dreamsoaked sheets.
Breathless, wet
with fear. Here

is your legacy
your Peace With Honour.
Here the hollow
trumpet, the dawn call;
still jungle, the blade
driven in

snapped off.
Parades of napalm.
A necklace of ears.
Fire in the hole.

PREMONITORY

I am beginning
to picture those beaches
that the sea
will never nuzzle

the wind diminishing
through leafless branches
and the defeated light.

Again I am becoming
one with winter
with the hollow road.

There will appear
a peopleless city
on the way to which
I shall pass by
all my constants.

An infinite fence.
The young mother
with her back to the sun.

The blank fields where
no mythical creature
can any longer feed.

NIGHT-LIGHT

Is that a sound
from outside someone
on the stairs something
moving in the mirror?
Surely not

but we still stay close
to our little glow
made smaller
by its wattage.

How ludicrous.
While we feign sleep
a small scarred man
parks his car in the dark,
shuffles down our street
with a half-filled sack.

He has room
for all of us in there.
He'll fold and pack
and rearrange things
make space for us beside

the spider's cry
the key to spring
the whispers of children.

NEW ORDER

Loud boys
bully boys, the world
a schoolyard
you swagger through.

Not too bright
but white, and that's enough
with a boot
and a stick
and a killing or two.

It's the song of the wasp
it's the old command
it's an aryan tune.

You salute in a vacuum.
We recognise you.
We already know
what you do.

The sad little flats.
The pictures of Hitler.
The mirrors you sneer into.

MELBOURNE BITTER

1. *'Six people are dead and ten others are injured*
after a gunman opened fire at random on motorists
in Hoddle Street, Clifton Hill, last night.'

Too long sick
of waiting
little room
been a good

boy bed made
linen pressed
frequent showers
clean boy

in the mirror
the gleaming
steel the black
clothes trigger

mirror good boy
rambo poster
facing me
turning he

can see a
good boy the
mirror is
watching me hope

he approves every
thing needs
polishing needs
to be spotless

can see in
hope he knows me
aiming and polishing
and checking

the calendar
a good boy aiming
polishing checking
the calendar.

2. *'Nine die in city rampage: Young killer leaps
from 11th floor to his death.'*

Nice snug
fit under my coat
right side
discreet. They

don't even glance
in the lobby.
Eleventh floor.
I see your face

in other faces
beneath desks
behind doors
it's alright it

must be like
(like in the dream)
it's alright I
finish I am

through the glass
(like the dream)
I don't
drop don't fall

I am held
in air the beautiful
street rushing up
to meet me.

3. *'Detectives believe the skeleton of a teenager*
found buried in a shallow grave in Thomastown
is that of the missing schoolgirl Karmein Chan.'

Cold
envelope the fold
around her
small-boned broken

cranium
shred of nightdress.
Machinery
above her its

steel teeth
eating through dirt
and gravel she has
not slept she

has been
awake beneath
this black crush
this city that

has taken in
the breath it can
never again
let out.

THE INVISIBLE CIRCUS

As we grow weary
an acrobat denies the net.
All around us

clowns sigh in dressing rooms
horses nod and tremble
in temporary stalls
ringmasters clear their throats
hold in their stomachs
stride out into the light.

As we close our eyes
a smiling woman
rests her head
in the lion's mouth.

As we sleep
a lean man is juggling fire.

Between our dreams
a dusty beast is leaving its cage.

VIRGINIA AND THE RIVER

A final cup.
A last glance
around these rooms
as the voices click
their tongues in your head.

It does not take long
to cross the wet meadow
and push through the bushes.
The march sky is bright
and cold, the bank
slippery and steep.

They are louder now.
There is no hesitation.
One firm step, the carefully
chosen stone in your coat

and voicelessly, delicate
as a lover the river
closes softly over you.

DEEP SOUTH

Hawks bank
over a deer carcass.
Shredded tyres curled up
by the roadside.
Old trucks. Bridges.
Dusk unfolding
in the valleys
blue hills still and distant
spilling into Virginia.

Before sundown
the blacks
gather in loose groups
not talking much.
Lost whites
suddenly less self-assured
on these unfamiliar streets
practise their averted gaze.
Don't stare honey.
Pretend it's not happening.
Look away, Dixieland.

They find the t.v. preacher
dead in a motel bed
alone, no note.
The seeds split open.
The terrible fruit blooms
ripens into suicide
is harvested by shotgun.
Next morning
after the cops have gone
the daymaid sponges him
off the mottled walls
with her eyes closed.

[56]

MULTIPLES

Curtains sewn
together. A sea

of clocks.
The crawlspace.
Bones

in the throat
dry and

unswallowable.
Basements.
Gloves.

The unseen.
Eclipses. Fog.

Two-way glass.
Scissors.
Rips

in the veil.
Let me explain.

[57]

BULGARIA

I can spell empty;
I've waited
on the cold stone.
There is the slow pool
and the blood tide
and the tiny cry.

I tell you
that deep inside men
a different river freezes.
Men's eyes open
onto mines
and wire
and deserted streets.

I am whispering
up through the ice
that deep inside men
lies no less desolate
a Europe.

ENCLOSURE

Late afternoon
the far peninsula
a quiet tide divides the bay.
Crickets stopping.
Shadows gathered in.

The garden waits
the curtains push
softly into the room.

Inside I am trying not
to breathe as her face
forms as she steps
through the mirror
I am trying

not to breathe
as she steps
out of the mirror.

GULF

The great cave.
Our small voices
calling the blood down

freeing the last birds
the stopped clock
the dark belly.

Nonage.
The white room.
An echo of feathers.

Will you
drop can you
any longer deny

the ripped cocoon
the bent wing
the signature

the frost
the red bell
the tiny light?

BLINDSIDE

The white season.
A chorus of mornings
before the worn hearth
the long light
the salt lick
of old wounds.

We carry our embers
through new woods
the cave-scent
on us we stop
at a curve
in the wall
out of sight
between sentinels.

There will not be long
to wait. Soon we
shall hear the urgent
traffic the message
the watchword
being whispered
along sentry posts
the code the signal
rich with warning

Listen for
Watch the
Be ready to

LEAVING ANTARCTICA

(fear)
the vertical ice
the lack of handholds

(need)
the unlikely climb
the frozen mountain

(promise)
the unlocked cabin
the thought of fire

(hope)
the unbroken snow with only
our tracks in it

(desire)
the flat place
the bright summit

(love)
the pick that slips
the delicious shiver
as the ropes go

SHELL

How well I melted
into the deaf night:
a mute tenement
a beautiful ruin

along the lampless
avenue on which
I crouch, haunches
sealed in concrete

elbows wedged
in delicate cement.
Each low window
a way in. Each loose

brick a symphony.
Each deliberate hollow
a selection of echoes
calling you

through slow shadows
and broken doors
and the corridors
of stone that are mine.